TRINITY GUILDHALL

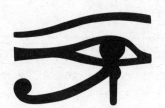

Sound at Sight

bass clef brass

Grades 1-8

First published in 2007 by:
Trinity College London
89 Albert Embankment
London SE1 7TP UK
E music@trinityguildhall.co.uk
www.trinityguildhall.co.uk

Printed in England by Halstan & Co. Ltd, Amersham, Bucks.

Trombone & Euphonium

• Grade 1   These pieces stay within a note range of a fifth in B♭ major.

1

10

11

12

Tuba

• Grade 1   These pieces stay within a note range of a fifth in E♭ major.

1

2

3

4

Trombone & Euphonium

● Grade 2

The $\frac{3}{4}$ time signature is introduced, along with simple ties and easy two-note slurs (for euphoniums only).

Tuba

• Grade 2   The ¾ time signature is introduced, along with simple ties and easy two-note slurs.

Trombone & Euphonium

• Grade 3
Quavers can be included from this grade, as well as larger slurred groups (for euphoniums only).

Tuba

• Grade 3   Quavers can be included from this grade, as well as larger slurred groups.

Trombone & Euphonium

• Grade 4

New keys, rhythms and articulations, plus an increased note range provide challenges at this grade. Trombonists should begin to observe slurs from this grade, using legato tonguing as appropriate.

Tuba

• Grade 4

New keys, rhythms and articulations, plus an increased note range provide challenges at this grade.

Trombone & Euphonium

• Grade 5
Semiquavers and the $\frac{6}{8}$ time signature are introduced at Grade 5.

Tuba

• Grade 5   Semiquavers and the $\frac{6}{8}$ time signature are introduced at Grade 5.

Trombone & Euphonium

• Grade 6   These pieces are slightly longer and may include $\frac{3}{8}$ time.

Tuba

• Grade 6

These pieces are slightly longer and may include $\frac{3}{8}$ time.

1

Allegro molto

2

Andante espressivo

3

Allegretto

4

Slow tango

23

5

Trombone & Euphonium

• Grade 7

A wider range of keys and time signatures are added at Grade 7 and a two octave note range is expected.

Tuba

• Grade 7
A wider range of keys and time signatures are added at Grade 7 and a two octave note range is expected.

Trombone & Euphonium

• Grade 8   Changing time signatures and a wider range of accidentals can be expected at Grade 8.

Tuba

• Grade 8   Changing time signatures and a wider range of accidentals can be expected at Grade 8.